D1319535

Auto Accident Claims:
The Ultimate Guide
Get the Maximum Settlement

Steven J. Schwartzapfel

Questions? Visit www.fightingforyou.com or call 800-966-4999.

Published by Lawyers Marketing Associates, Inc., P.O. Box 728, Oxford, NC, 27565.Contact the publisher at (919) 637-9144 for more information.

AUTO ACCIDENT CLAIMS: THE ULTIMATE GUIDE

Get the Maximum Settlement

Author: Steven J. Schwartzapfel

ISBN 978-0-9886452-0-2

Questions? Visit www.fightingforyou.com or call 800-966-4999.

Table of Contents

Questions? Visit www.fightingforyou.com or call 800-966-4999.

Introduction

Thank you for buying or requesting this book. I am so confident that you will find this book helpful that it comes with a 100 percent satisfaction guarantee.

No one ever thinks they will be seriously injured; however, according to the National Highway Transportation Safety Administration's latest data, each and every day over 100 people die in auto accidents, and more than 7,500 are injured.[1] In fact, you and everyone you know or care about will, on average, be involved in three accidents during your or their lifetime. If you or someone you care about has been injured in an accident, chances are you are worrying about what to do next. It is normal to feel angry, confused, frustrated, and depressed. Most people don't know what to do or who to trust. It seems everyone has an opinion, but how do you know it is the right advice? How can you risk you or your family's health or financial future?

You may be asking yourself, "Who will pay my medical bills and lost wages? Are there any time limits to apply for benefits? Who is going to pay for my car? Do I put a claim in with my insurance company or the other person's? The insurance company keeps calling; can I trust them? Do I have a case, and how much is it worth? Are there any time limits to file a claim or lawsuit? Do I need a lawyer?"

---

[1] https://crashstats.nhtsa.dot.gov

If any of these questions sound familiar, read on. This book answers all of these questions and more. Having this knowledge will reduce your anxiety and give you a certain comfort level on what to do next.

This book is primarily about auto accidents; however, much of the information contained in this book applies to many other claims, including construction site accidents, slip, trip, and fall accidents, medical malpractice injuries, defective product injuries, workers' compensation claims, etc. Regardless of how you were injured, this book provides valuable information that you may find helpful.

The Book Includes:
- Secrets insurance companies would rather you not know
- Personal injury myths
- How insurance companies operate
- How to protect yourself
- The claims and litigation process
- Frequently asked questions
- Questions to ask before hiring a lawyer

Important Disclaimer

This book is not intended to nor does it provide legal advice. This book is intended as a public service for consumers. **DO NOT** take or rely on anything in this book to be legal advice.

Any lawyer, however well-intentioned, who gives legal advice without devoting the requisite time and attention to understanding the specifics of your case is doing the public a disservice.

Who Am I, and Why Did I Write This Book?

My name is Steven Schwartzapfel. I am an attorney. For over thirty-five years it has been my privilege and honor to represent consumers and their families who have been seriously injured, maimed, disabled, or killed as a result of someone else's wrongdoing.

As long as I can remember, I have wanted to help people. Growing up, I was a Boy Scout and became an Eagle Scout. Doing a good turn daily and helping other people not only comes naturally to me, it is in my DNA; it is who I am.

In my first job out of law school, I worked for an insurance company defending accident cases. I learned firsthand the tricks, tactics, and strategies the insurance company would engage in to delay and deny legitimate claims. I saw the lengths to which the insurance company would go to avoid paying medical bills and other claims. I learned that the insurance company's sole purpose was to make profits for its shareholders, not to pay claims.

Needless to say, the job was less than satisfying, and after gaining as much knowledge and experience as I could working on behalf of insurance companies, I left to help protect the rights of people who could not fight for themselves.

That's not to mean that all insurance company adjusters and defense attorneys are bad people. It is easy to become cynical when they see frivolous claims. I hold in high regard those few insurance company adjusters and defense attorneys who have

3

not become cynical, those who can still distinguish and value human dignity and understand how quality of life is diminished when someone is seriously injured, maimed or disabled.

Insurance companies know and count on many people giving up their legal rights and the money and benefits they are entitled to. The insurance company's tactics of setting up roadblocks and obstacles and of stalling and delaying are not by accident, but rather by design. Remember, insurance companies exist to make profit for their shareholders, and every penny they don't pay out in claims they keep.

Having represented thousands of consumers injured as a result of someone else's wrongdoing, usually due to someone else's failure to follow the rules, we are seeing a dramatic and alarming trend where hard-working New Yorkers are being taken advantage of by insurance companies.

With the recent changes in the law and the ways in which insurance companies are processing claims, it is important that you get the help you need as quickly as possible. The last thing you need is to have the insurance company take advantage of you during this most difficult time in your life.

Another concerning trend is the rise in certain lawyer advertising. Some lawyers are making promises that are meaningless, such as "our no-fee guarantee," or equating your injury to "cash, cash, cash." The law in New York is clear: there is no attorney fee unless there is a recovery. Frivolous lawsuits and frivolous defenses hurt everyone. They clog up the courts and delay legitimate claims from getting to court.

The hiring of an attorney is an extremely important decision that you should be able to make without pressure. This book helps you decide if you need an attorney and provides the important steps you should take prior to hiring an attorney to best represent you and your family.

I wrote this book with one goal in mind: If someone I loved and cared about, whether it was my mother, father, sister, brother, wife, child, or best friend, were in an accident, what are the most important things I would want them to know? The book provides information consumers need before hiring an attorney or speaking with the insurance company.

It is my genuine hope and desire that this book helps you avoid making the costly mistakes that can ruin your and your family's financial future. Even if we do not accept your case, we still want to educate you so you don't fall prey to the insurance company's tactics, or hire a TV lawyer who lacks the skill, experience, knowledge, and resources to get you the money and benefits you are entitled to. This book allows you to make an informed decision immediately and informs you how best to go about protecting your rights.

Questions? Visit www.fightingforyou.com or call 800-966-4999.

Let's Get Started

What is a personal injury claim?

To begin, it will help you to understand a little bit about personal injury law. If another person or entity has injured you as a result of wrongdoing, you may have a personal injury claim. A personal injury is the physical and mental harm suffered by one person caused by the fault, carelessness, negligence, or wrongdoing of another.

As an example, if while stopped at a red light another driver rear-ends you but the only damage is to your car, then you would have a claim for property damage only. You would not have a claim for personal injuries regardless of the amount of damage to your car.

However, if both you and your car sustained damage then you may have claims for both personal injuries and property damage. In the event you suffered both personal injuries and property damage, your own insurance company may take care of your property damage claim and car rental expenses depending on your policy.

Do I have a case?

Anytime someone dies or suffers injuries as a result of someone else's wrongdoing that person may have a case. There are many factors involved when an attorney decides whether to accept a case. Just because a lawyer tells a person it's not a case he would accept, this does not mean the person doesn't have a case. A different lawyer may reach a different conclusion.

Several years ago, a lawyer called me asking if I could help a young man who had become quadriplegic. He had no recollection of how the accident occurred. No one else was present at the time and there were no witnesses to the accident. The young man had already contacted three different lawyers who told him he didn't have a case. The fact is, he did have a case; however, the law has become so highly specialized that even lawyers claiming to do personal injury law often lack the skill, experience, expertise, and financial resources necessary to fully investigate and prosecute a case against major insurance companies, corporate giants, and municipalities.

In the event a lawyer tells you it's not a case, seek another opinion immediately, as there are time limits, referred to as statute of limitations, within which you can bring a claim or file a lawsuit. Similarly, if you are injured at work, there are some time limits within which you must give notice to your employer and file a claim. Failure to do so within the prescribed time limits can result in losing all rights, money, and benefits you may otherwise be entitled to.

Don't simply accept one lawyer's opinion. Like most things in life, law has become highly complex and specialized. You don't want a lawyer that handles real estate closings, matrimonial law, family law, commercial transactions, criminal law, immigration, elder law, and an occasional run-of-the-mill auto accident giving you advice if you or a family member is seriously injured.

Questions? Visit www.fightingforyou.com or call 800-966-4999.

There may be multiple causes, theories of liability, and multiple defendants responsible for the incident. What at first glance may appear to be simply an auto accident may also be the result of an employer who negligently hired a driver with a history of prior tickets, arrests, and convictions. Or, it may be the result of an automotive manufacturer defect; the result of a failure to have performed a proper New York State vehicle inspection; or a product recall, such as a defective tire, a flawed accelerator, defective brakes or defective steering mechanism. Additionally, it could be from the repair shop failing to properly repair the vehicle or the result of a highway design defect, improper highway signage, or highway draining. As you can see, the list of possible causes and responsible parties even in what appears to be a simple auto accident goes on and on.

It is imperative that you retain a lawyer with experience, expertise, and a proven record of success handling the particular claim or type of accident that you were involved in and that caused your injuries.

Are there any time limits to make a claim or file a lawsuit that apply in a personal injury case?
Yes. There may be one or more Statutes of Limitations that may apply to your case. Your claim must be filed before the expiration of any Statute of Limitation or your claim may be forever barred. Note that some Statutes of Limitation are as short as thirty (30) days. It is important that you act without delay. If you were injured, we strongly recommend you contact a highly credentialed and well-qualified lawyer immediately. Your lawyer may file a claim or a lawsuit against the wrongdoers for all the harms and losses you suffered.

What is a wrongful death claim?

A wrongful death case means someone else's wrongdoing causes injuries that result in the death of another. The laws regarding a wrongful death case can be significantly different from state to state. In New York, there is no right for family members to recover for their pain and suffering.

There is an exception to this rule known as the "zone of danger" exception, which recognizes the right of a family member who was in the zone of danger (and could have been killed) to recover for their pain and suffering even if they were not injured.

Florida and Pennsylvania, on the other hand, recognize and allow recovery for the pain and suffering of the survivors without any zone of danger requirement. It is especially important to consult with a highly experienced attorney who is familiar with the specialized wrongful death laws.

Types of Personal Injury Cases

Car, truck, bus, and motorcycle accidents, construction accidents, workplace injuries, slip, trip, and fall accidents, medical malpractice, dangerous defective products, and drugs can all be the cause of personal injuries and wrongful death. Examples include:

1. **Car, bus, taxi, truck, and motorcycle accidents**
   These common accidents usually occur when one driver fails to follow the rules and/or fails to pay attention and hits the other vehicle or person.

2. **Construction accidents and workplace injuries**

Questions? Visit www.fightingforyou.com or call 800-966-4999.

Examples of these accidents include injuries sustained when a worker falls from scaffolding, a ladder, or any height, suffers injury due to falling objects, or trips and falls due to garbage or debris on the ground, or due to the failure to have been given any safety equipment or protective device.

3. **Slip, trip, and fall accidents**
    Falls on sidewalks or steps that are broken, cracked, raised, or slippery due to a failure to maintain, repair, and/or clear snow, ice, garbage, or debris in a timely manner.

4. **Medical malpractice**
    Medical, doctor, or hospital mistakes or errors, such as failing to timely diagnose cancer or failing to perform a timely and proper delivery resulting in birth injuries, such as Cerebral and Erbs Palsy.

5. **Defective products and drugs**
    Injuries due to drugs and products whereby the manufacturer knew or should have known its products could injure or kill and failed to warn the public or engaged in deceit, distortion, and deception, such as certain tobacco, asbestos, medical drug companies, and device manufacturers.

In order to successfully bring a personal injury claim, you must prove that the other person or entity was careless, negligent, or at fault, and that their negligent conduct was a cause of your injuries.

So, Where Do I Start?

If you, a family member, or best friend sustained a serious injury in an accident, you may feel frustrated, angry, and overwhelmed. One moment you were healthy, enjoying the simple things in life we all take for granted, such as getting up in the morning after a full night of sleep, getting out of bed, taking a shower, getting dressed by yourself, having breakfast, going to work or school, or simply engaging in your usual routine. Then you were involved in an accident as a result of someone else's wrongdoing. Because someone else failed to follow the rules, your life as you knew it is forever changed.

Now you can't remember the last time you slept through the night. Getting up in the morning and out the door used to take minutes, now it's a lengthy ordeal—if you can get out at all.

You're in pain and discomfort and require ongoing medical care and attention. It is a revolving door of doctors, therapies, and medication. You can't do what you did before.

You can't work and don't know when, if ever, you'll be able to return to work or return to your usual and ordinary routine. You were once mobile, now you're not. You once had a productive life, now other than doctor's visits, you're alone and isolated. Bills are piling up; you may be angry, irritable, depressed, frustrated, and overwhelmed. The whole family is paying the price all because of someone else's carelessness, negligence, and wrongdoing. If that person had only followed the rules, had paid attention, had done what he or she was supposed to have done and acted in a reasonable manner, none of this would have happened.

11

You may have no idea what to do next or what money and benefits you are entitled to. You may be asking yourself, "Can I trust my insurance company? Can I collect no-fault benefits, workers' compensation or Social Security disability benefits? Whose insurance company is going to pay to repair the damage to my car?"

The questions seem endless and it's normal to feel confused and overwhelmed. Most lawyers do not know these answers unless their practice area concentrates specifically on personal injury cases. You may also want to know if you can afford a lawyer or know how to find the best possible attorney. This book will hopefully reduce your stress and frustration and provide the answers you are looking for now to best protect you and your family.

Secrets Insurance Companies Would Rather You Not Know

In the following sections, I will address some of the tactics that insurance companies use to limit payouts on claims. I'll explain some of the myths out there, how insurance companies operate, and ways you can protect yourself by understanding what the insurance company is NOT telling you.

7 Personal Injury Myths

1. MYTH: The insurance adjuster is on your side and is there to help you. TRUTH: The insurance adjuster is paid to protect the interests of the insurance company.
2. MYTH: The accident wasn't your fault, so some insurance company will automatically pay for the property damage to your car, your medical bills, your lost wages, and your losses and harms suffered. TRUTH: Insurance companies exist to make a profit. They do so by denying, delaying, or paying out as little as possible on claims. The insurance company will usually fight you every step of the way.
3. MYTH: When you are in an accident and the insurance company calls and asks for a recorded statement, you must give them one or they will not settle with you. TRUTH: The insurance company would like you to give a recorded statement so they can use it against you later. New York law does not require you to give a recorded statement. Do not give any statement to anyone until you have consulted a lawyer.

4. MYTH: The accident wasn't your fault, so if you give the insurance company a recorded or written statement they will pay for property damage and medical bills. TRUTH: The insurance company will take whatever steps are necessary to deny your claim and limit payouts.

5. MYTH: The insurance company will make a fair and reasonable settlement offer. TRUTH: The insurance company is under no obligation to make any settlement offer. They will dangle the possibility of an offer only to obtain as much information as they can gather to use against you later. If a settlement offer is made, it will be below the actual value of your case.

6. MYTH: The insurance company will not offer or pay more money if you hire a lawyer. TRUTH: The insurance company's own research shows settlements in cases where the injured person is represented by a lawyer are significantly higher and the client receives more money even after payment of attorney fees.

7. MYTH: The accident wasn't your fault and you sustained such serious injuries that if you just tell the insurance company adjuster or go to court and tell the jury your story, they will feel badly for you and give you money to compensate you for all your losses. TRUTH: Jurors are not generous. Focus groups have proven that jurors are often skeptical, cynical, and reluctant to believe the injured party. Jurors have become desensitized to blood and gore after seeing so much of it on TV, social media, and in movies. It has become increasingly difficult for an injured person to recover the full value of his or her losses without having retained a highly experienced and well-qualified lawyer.

Questions? Visit www.fightingforyou.com or call 800-966-4999.

How Insurance Companies Operate

Insurance companies are corporations in business for one purpose and one purpose only—to make profit for their shareholders. The insurance companies are not in existence to pay you one penny more – that's right, not one cent more than they have to.

More than 35 years ago, I worked as an attorney representing the insurance company defending personal injury claims. I can tell you, having firsthand knowledge, that the insurance company will do everything within their power to stall, delay, or deny your claim. The insurance company knows that their tactics will further delay your case and increase their likelihood of success. Having experienced counsel by your side can make all the difference between your success and theirs.

The insurance company representatives and lawyers will strive to make a simple accident ambiguous, confusing, and complex. The longer the case drags on, the more money the insurance company makes earning interest on their money. The insurance company also knows it will cost you or your lawyer money to prosecute or try the case.

In New York State, the minimum policy limit is $25,000 dollars. Rarely is there any incentive for the insurance company to offer $25,000 early on regardless of how badly injured or disabled you are. The insurance company knows the insurance policy limit is the highest amount they will ever have to pay anyone. There is absolutely no reason for the insurance company to have to pay you early on when they can pay you years later and

15

earn interest on the money. If the injured person is elderly, the insurance company will never admit it, but they actually hope the person dies before the case ever gets to trial.

Stalling, delaying, and denying claims works to the insurance company's benefit, not yours. The insurance companies have highly experienced and skilled lawyers and investigators to protect their interests, to minimize their exposure, and to pay you as little – or nothing – if possible. And they train their insurance adjusters to take advantage of claimants who have not yet retained an attorney and have no idea of how much money their claim is worth.

The insurance companies and corporate wrongdoers have tremendous resources and have spent countless dollars figuring out every possible trick, trap, and tactic not to pay out money in claims. Whether by spending billions of dollars on lobbyists, public relation firms, think tanks and funding political action committees (PACS), or simply by running ads and articles to distort the facts, poison the minds of American consumers and juries, push their anti-consumer tort reform agenda to limit consumers' access to the civil justice system, or limit trial by a jury—make no mistake about it—insurance companies and corporate wrongdoers do not want to be held accountable.

The insurance companies have also learned that the sooner they can investigate and begin processing the claim, the less money they will have to pay out. Many insurance companies now have a twenty-four-hour rule. It is their goal to make contact with the claimant and take statements within twenty-four hours of the accident. Some insurance companies even

16

have adjusters in vehicles on standby waiting for a call to be notified of an accident. The adjusters now drive right to the accident scene or even to the hospital to begin defending the claim.

These insurance company investigators and adjusters are highly trained. They act concerned, compassionate, friendly, and helpful. They may be neighbors, belong to local churches or temples, coach little league or soccer, belong to the same civic group or business networking group, and they may appear to be wonderful people. Don't be fooled—their sole purpose is to protect the insurance company, not you.

The insurance company is under no obligation to tell you your legal rights. Often, they will falsely tell you that you must give a written or recorded statement or fill out a form if you want the insurance company to pay for your property damage or anything else. Then they use the statement against you as grounds not to pay. **Do not speak with any insurance company representative until you have spoken to a lawyer.**

Insurance companies will often tell you not to hire a lawyer, or that you don't need one. They are well aware of the studies done that prove that a person with a lawyer receives, on average, three-and-one-half times more money than a person without a lawyer. Even after paying attorney fees, the claimant often receives more than double the amount of money he or she would have otherwise received.

Most recently, we have noticed insurance company representatives also showing up at the hospitals and

17

accompanying clients to doctor visits, demanding to be present during examinations. The latter are nurse practitioners whose purpose is to intimidate the client, the doctor's office, and staff. Their mission is to cut off and deny benefits as quickly as possible and then to testify against the client if the case proceeds to trial. They never tell the client that they have no legal right to even be there.

One of the insurance company's primary goals is to obtain a written or recorded statement as soon as they can. They know the quicker they get a statement, the better they can defend or deny a claim. Unless you have been involved in an accident, you can't imagine how stressful, surreal, and upsetting the whole thing is—especially if family members were hurt, injured, or killed. Your entire body, system, and mind may be in a state of shock. The accident may have knocked you out or caused you to black out.

We've had clients who have broken their legs, had their bones sticking out, and, while in the hospital on pain medication, the insurance company adjuster shows up trying to take a statement.

Even if you are seriously injured, unconscious, suffering from catastrophic injuries and in shock, it does not stop the insurance company from calling or showing up at the hospital or your home demanding a statement.

The insurance companies know the importance and value of immediately investigating and processing the claim. The insurance company is also aware that immediately after the accident, not only is the client often dazed, confused, and in a state of shock, but many injuries have a latency period where the neck, back, shoulder, and/or knee gets progressively worse, not better, as days, weeks, and months go by.

Medical research proves that the full extent of certain injuries is usually unknown at the time of the accident. The insurance company also knows that when a person is lying in bed in excruciating pain with broken bones they usually are not focusing or aware that other parts of their body are bruised, sore, battered, swollen, and injured.

The adjuster has training in basic psychology on how to phrase questions to get you to not even mention, or to minimize, the nature of injuries, pain, or impact of an injury. For instance, the insurance company adjuster or investigator typically asks questions and writes out "your" statement for you to sign.

The adjustor may ask you, "No other parts of your body hurt you at this time?" However, the adjuster may only write down "no other injuries or complaints" and omit from your statement "at this time." In addition, adjusters will do everything within their power to phrase questions to make it appear that you are fully or partially at fault for the accident.

Remember, you are under no obligation to give any statement. The old adage is true, "Anything you say can and will be used against you." Actually, we have found that anything you say can and will be *misconstrued* and used against you. Remember you are under no obligation to answer any questions. Do not fill out or sign any forms without advice from experienced legal

19

counsel. **Do not allow** anyone to intimidate you into making any decision or doing anything without first speaking to a lawyer. Politely but firmly tell the insurance company adjuster you will give a statement but not at this time. Do so only after you've spoken to your lawyer.

It is not uncommon for insurance company adjusters to tell you they will not pay your medical bills or property damage, or pay any money or any more money once you get a lawyer. This is simply not true.

Worst of all, do not, under any circumstances, accept any money from the insurance company without speaking to a lawyer. **Do not** enter into any agreements with the insurance company. **Do not** sign anything or settle your claim without first speaking to a lawyer. Insurance companies are notorious for telling clients they are going to give them a check for property damage and/or miscellaneous expenses, and then have the clients unknowingly sign a general release, releasing the defendants and forever giving up all rights, including the right to past and future medical expenses, lost wages, pain, and suffering.

We have had clients, especially our Spanish-speaking clients, told by insurance company adjusters that they are receiving money for their car and miscellaneous expenses. Only later did they find out that they gave up their right to sue for serious personal injuries.

We've had clients still hospitalized from their injuries, contacted and visited in the hospitals by these very friendly, pleasant, and concerned adjusters for the sole purpose of trying to settle their cases cheaply. The truth was the insurance company paid them what seemed like a lot of money, had them sign general releases, but in reality paid them less than 10 percent of what the case was really worth. We have been successful in setting aside the fraudulently obtained releases and settled the cases for ten times the amount originally paid.

The law does not allow any insurance company to settle a child's case without a court order. The law defines a child as any person under the age of eighteen. If you or someone you know received money from an insurance company for or on behalf of a child, without a lawyer and without going to court, you were a victim of fraud by the insurance company. Contact a lawyer immediately. You did nothing wrong. You can keep the money, and you and your child may be entitled to collect more money. No judge and no court of law are sympathetic when an insurance company takes advantage of children.

How You Can Protect Yourself

After reading about some of the techniques insurance companies use to protect their bottom line, you may be asking yourself what *you* can do to protect *your* bottom line. After years of handling auto accident cases, I have seen some common mistakes that injured people make that can be fatal to their claims. This section covers mistakes you should avoid in order to maximize your settlement and protect yourself. These are valuable secrets that the big insurance companies hoped you'd never know!

Fatal Mistake 1: Not Taking Immediate Action at the Accident Scene to Preserve Your Rights

- **If you have an automobile collision, stop immediately,** but do not block traffic. New York law requires that you not leave the scene of an accident, even a minor one, without first stopping to see whether there are damages or injuries.

- **Do not stand between or behind the vehicles.** If you cannot immediately move all vehicles out of traffic lanes, warn oncoming automobiles by setting out road flares, turning on hazard lights, or raising the hood or trunk of your vehicle and other vehicles. **Remain in your vehicle if it is safe to do so.**

- **Call for an ambulance if there are injuries.** Assist anyone who may be injured, but be careful not to move seriously injured persons unless necessary to remove them from further danger.

- **Keep calm, don't argue, don't accuse anyone, and don't admit fault.** Things you say immediately after the accident can be used against you later, so don't discuss the accident with the other driver and don't take the blame for it or accuse the other driver of causing the collision.

- **Call 911 and cooperate with the investigating officers.** Do not allow the other driver to talk you into not contacting the police. In many cities, the police will not come to the scene of a minor collision. Let the police make this decision—call them anyway. If a police officer does come to the scene, ask him or her to make a written accident report and give you the incident number of the report. Be sure to get the names and badge numbers of the investigating officers. Also be sure you know which agency the officer is representing. He or she could be a city, county, town, or village police officer, a county sheriff's deputy, or a state trooper.

  If filed, a police report should be available for you to pick up a few days after the collision. Ask the officer where you can get the report. If you don't have a lawyer to do this for you, get a copy of the report yourself. Check the report very carefully to be sure all details are correct. Sometimes the investigating officer will correct an error in the report if you point out the error quickly. After some time passes, though, the officer will not be able to remember the details, and will have to go by what was written on the report.

- **Get as much information as possible at the scene.** Make written notes of the names, addresses, phone numbers

Questions? Visit www.fightingforyou.com or call 800-966-4999.

(mobile, home, and work), and license plate numbers of all parties involved, including any witnesses to the accident, or, simply use your cell phone camera to take photos of licenses, registrations, and insurance cards.

- **Photograph all damages and the accident scene.** Remember you can use your cell phone to take pictures and video. At the accident scene, if you can do so safely, take photos and videos of the entire accident scene, including the street scene, traffic control devices (i.e., stop signs, yield signs, stoplights), skid marks, and any physical objects the vehicle may have struck (i.e., guardrails, light poles, etc.). Even photograph the other drivers, passengers, and witnesses, if possible. If you have an injury and cannot take photos, ask someone to do it for you. A short video of the entire scene can be extremely helpful in showing a clear depiction of the relationship of vehicles and objects. If your injury occurred at a place of business or was the result of a dangerous condition, similarly, take photos and video. In an accident at a business or store, take photos of the manager and any employees you reported it to or anyone that witnessed the dangerous conditions.

- **Exchange information with the other parties.** Always keep a pen and paper in your vehicle. If you have a cell phone, take a picture of the other driver's insurance card and license. If not, write down as much as possible from the other driver's insurance card and driver's license. Write down the license plate numbers and the color, make, and model of the other vehicles. Get all contact information from other parties and witnesses, including full names, home, work and cell phone numbers, home and work address, etc.

- **Do not admit fault.** Do not make any statements regarding injuries except to the police or paramedics.
    - ✓ Call us at 800-966-4999.
    - ✓ Visit our website at www.fightingforyou.com for your free accident information card that will hold your insurance card and registration and sets forth all the information you will need to obtain.

- **If you feel unsafe at the accident scene, remain in your vehicle** with the doors locked until the police arrive.

Questions? Visit www.fightingforyou.com or call 800-966-4999.

Fatal Mistake 2: Not Documenting Everything That Happens After the Accident Occurs

- **The importance of documentation**

  When an insurance adjuster receives your claim for settlement, or when your case comes to trial, here's a fact of life: It's not what actually happened, but only what you can prove happened. You're going to have to prove it was the other driver's fault and prove your damages. How? You prove your facts and damages by documenting everything you possibly can. We've already talked about documenting everything at the scene of the collision or accident. But the need for documentation only begins at that point. It doesn't end until your case is completed.

- **Write down what happened**

  It's amazing how quickly we forget the pain and suffering we have gone through. Written words help us remember. That's why we take a shopping list to the grocery store!

  One of the first things to do after an injury is to go home and write out everything you can remember about the accident itself. You'll remember things after you get home that you forgot to write down or didn't have a chance to write down at the scene.

- **Keep a diary of your injuries**

  Keep a detailed pain diary. There is a strange phenomenon regarding pain. When you are in pain, it consumes you. That is all that you can think about. Ever have a toothache or burn yourself? It's not just your tooth or finger that is in pain; it's your entire body. When you're no longer in pain, you forget that you ever were in pain. If you can't write because of your injuries, dictate your thoughts to a family member or have a friend write them down for you. This simple secret becomes a powerful tool to maximize your financial recovery. It is important to make your diary entries as frequently as possible. A summary at the end of each month will not be nearly as accurate as daily entries.

- **Keep your receipts**

  Like it or not, dealing with insurance companies is like a giant paper shuffle. Documentation is the key to keeping an insurance company honest and on their toes. If you want reimbursement for an expense, you will first have to show proof of the expense. For example, if, because of your injuries, you have to hire someone to cut your grass or clean your house, you need receipts to prove you spent the money. If you have to travel to a doctor's office, keep transportation receipts or keep track of the mileage. If you pay for prescriptions or medications, keep the receipts. It is amazing how many of these reimbursable expenses slip through the cracks, unless you make notes, keep receipts, and bring them to the adjuster's attention.

- **Keep detailed notes and get names**

  Document all conversations with insurance company representatives; also get names, phone numbers, and job titles of everyone you talk with. If you have a problem with someone from an insurance company, ask to speak to that person's supervisor.

- **Take steps before you talk to the insurance company**
  It is our recommendation that you never speak with any insurance company adjuster until you speak with an attorney.

- **Keep a calendar of your doctor visits**
  I promise that you will not remember every date and time you saw a doctor or therapist. Keep a calendar and mark each medical visit or other significant event. Write down what time you left the house, how long you were at the doctor's office (including wait times), and the time you returned home. Keep a record of how long you had to stay confined to bed or to your home, use a wheelchair or walker, when you got crutches, how long you were on crutches, when you got off the crutches, when you stopped wearing a neck brace, and so on.

  ✓ Get the correct addresses and phone numbers of all doctors or clinics you visit. Pick up business cards when you are in their offices.

  ✓ Save all your pill bottles, casts, braces, and any other similar items you receive from your doctors. Remember, it is one thing to read about all the medication you require because of your injuries and pain, it is quite another to see all of the many, many pill bottles and medication you required due to an injury.

- **Document your lost wages**

  The insurance company is not going to take you at your word. If you want to recover any earnings you lost because of this accident, you're going to have to prove to the insurance company every penny you lost. The normal way to prove lost earnings is with a statement from your employer. However, the insurance company may also want to see copies of your paychecks and/or W-2's. If you are self-employed, or paid on commission, it can be a real challenge to convince the insurance company of your lost income. The insurance company may want to see copies of your tax returns for periods of time before and after the injury.

- **Keep a photographic record**

  I said earlier that a picture is worth a thousand words. This is also true when it comes to injuries. Pictures can be the difference between an average verdict or settlement and a great verdict or settlement. The right photograph can be a very powerful tool in motivating the insurance company to make a fair settlement offer or a jury to return a just verdict. Video is also a very effective tool. Video can show the complete picture of the accident scene and show how your injuries have impacted your usual and ordinary activities of daily living. It can also dramatically highlight the most important aspects of your case. If your injuries result in severe bruising or scarring, it's important to get clear photographs to document your injury. The more effectively you can do that, the better you can prove your case. So, take photos of your injuries and make a photo record of your stay in the hospital. If your injuries created a serious scar, it is vital to get clear, close-up pictures to show the details of the scarring. When in doubt, photograph it!

- **File a workers' compensation claim, if applicable**
  If you were actively engaged in a work-related activity at the time of the accident when you were injured, you may have the right to file a workers' compensation claim. It is important to file a workers' compensation claim in addition to a no-fault claim. Workers' compensation provides reimbursement of your lost wages, medical benefits, and other benefits. It is also important to let your doctors know if the injury is work-related so they can document their records and reports.

- **Hire an attorney early on**
  If you hire a lawyer early in the process, the law firm should be able to help with the necessary photographs and video. For instance, at Schwartzapfel Lawyers, we have at our disposal investigators, accident reconstruction experts, highway design experts, professional photographers, and videographers. They will, among other things, take photographs of your vehicle and of any cuts, bruises, or scars you have suffered. We also recommend a video of a day in the life of our clients who have sustained catastrophic injuries, going through their daily routine, as well as physical rehabilitation and gruesome procedures such as debriding or changing of dressing in burn cases or wound care.

Fatal Mistake 3: Not Going to the Emergency Room, Not Seeing Your Doctor, or Not Cooperating Completely with Your Doctors

- **Get to the emergency room or urgent care center quickly.** Make sure you are seen in the ER or an urgent care center – even if you are in minimal pain or discomfort. After representing many thousands of injured clients, I can say with near certainty that you will feel worse the day after the accident, and you will probably feel even worse the second and third days. It is not uncommon for clients to feel worse weeks, months, or years after the accident, as their injuries worsen with time.

Don't assume that just because you don't feel immediate and excruciating pain, you are not injured. If you break your arm, you'll know it right away! But if you sprain your neck, shoulder, knee, or back, you may at first only feel minor pain, aches, or discomfort. It may be weeks, months, or longer before that minor pain or ache is no longer minor but has rendered you disabled. Then, by the time you get to see your doctor, you're in excruciating pain. It's important to go to the emergency room, urgent care center, or see your doctor immediately after the accident. Share all your complaints of pain – even if they are minimal – and let your doctor document all the parts of your body that hurt. It is important that doctors verify and document all your complaints of pain immediately after an accident. Start some preventive care, so that your injuries may not be as severe as if you had waited. Although the medical literature is clear that certain injuries have a delayed onset before the

31

full nature and extent of the injury manifests itself, it doesn't stop the insurance company from claiming your injuries occurred elsewhere.

- **There's another reason to see a doctor immediately.** After an accident, many people try and tough it out, even though they may be in great pain and in need of medical care. Most people are embarrassed to ride in an ambulance. The insurance company will use your refusal or failure to go to the emergency room against you later. The adjuster, defense attorneys, and juries believe that if you were "really" hurt in the accident, you would have gone to the emergency room. Also, an insurance adjuster or defense attorney may argue that the failure to see a doctor immediately indicates that an injury must have occurred elsewhere and is not from this accident. The longer you wait for medical treatment, the more difficult it will be to convince the insurance company adjuster, judge, or jury that your injuries are causally related to the accident.

- **Tell your doctor about all your aches and pains.** We hear insurance adjusters and defense attorneys say all the time that since the client didn't complain about some specific injury the first time he or she saw a doctor, the injury must have happened elsewhere and at a later time. It's just human nature to tell the doctor about what hurts the worst and not mention the little aches and pains. But what often happens is that instead of those little aches or pains improving, they get progressively worse.

Questions? Visit www.fightingforyou.com or call 800-966-4999.

It's not uncommon for minor neck, back, shoulder, or knee pain to become so bad that our clients often require surgery months or years later, after conservative treatment and therapy fail. It is imperative that you tell the doctor every single problem you have, no matter how insignificant or minor it may seem to you. Always tell the doctor or therapist about every pain or problem you have. Don't try to diagnose yourself—you may make your injury and your case worse.

- **Do not miss your doctor appointments!**
  You need to make a commitment to your health and to your recovery by keeping your doctor appointments, even if it is time consuming to do so. There is almost never a good reason or excuse to miss a doctor appointment, because by missing one doctor appointment, you are saying to the insurance company that you don't hurt and that your injury doesn't matter that much. Each time you go to the doctor and report that you are still having pain, your doctor makes an entry in the records. It is important for your doctor to have up-to-date information on your condition. Not going to the doctor is a good way to "prove" that you are not hurting and that you don't care. If you don't care, the doctor may not care, and the insurance company and jury will certainly not care. It is very important for you to work hard to get well, and to do this it is critical that you go to every one of your medical appointments. Your failure to do so will irreparably harm the value of your injuries and the amount of money you may ultimately receive.

- **Insurance companies will claim that if you are not seeing a doctor you must not have sustained serious injuries** or that you must have recovered from your injuries, regardless of the truth, regardless of how badly you're injured, and regardless of whether you are still in pain.

- **Be sure to give each of your doctors an explanation of how your accident occurred.** Doctors may see hundreds of accident victims per year. Your medical records are a key piece of evidence in pursuing your personal injury claim. Therefore, it's important to tell all your doctors and other medical care providers about your accident. Tell the doctors if the car you were driving or were a passenger in was hit in the rear, if you lost consciousness or if your car's airbags deployed. If the doctor has an understanding of how the accident occurred, he or she can better understand the nature of the injuries that resulted from the accident, make a better diagnosis of your injuries, and devise a better treatment plan. (As mentioned above, tell your doctor if your injuries happened when you were actively engaged in a work-related activity.)

- **Always be honest about any prior accidents and injuries you have had.**
  The doctor needs this information in order to distinguish your old injuries from your new injuries. The doctor can determine the extent to which this accident has aggravated your prior injuries. Please note: Denying prior injuries can hurt your case, not help it.

- **Always be truthful with your lawyer** regarding prior accidents and injuries. Your failure to do so can be fatal to your accident claim.

- **Always be honest with your doctors.**
  Don't ever exaggerate or minimize your injuries. They are just trying to help you and you need to cooperate and be truthful with them so you get the treatment you require. If you minimize an injury, your doctor may not note it in your file; this may cause problems with your case down the road. Also cooperate by doing what your doctors tell you to do. As best you can, follow your doctors' instructions. And be sure the doctors know what you are doing outside the doctor's office. In other words, don't let the doctor think you're staying home and resting in bed if you're actually working. Keep your doctor informed so that the doctor's records reflect the truth.

Fatal Mistake 4: Giving Statements, Signing Papers, or Accepting Any Insurance Company Settlement Offer without First Getting Legal Advice

- **Do not give any statements**, written or oral, to anyone concerning your accident or injuries without first speaking with a lawyer. Anything you say will be misconstrued and used against you. If the insurance company adjuster wants a statement, it's not to help you. The statement will be used against you at a later time. If you feel uncomfortable saying, "I'm not going to give a statement, thank you, and goodbye," tell the insurance company adjuster you will be happy to give a statement once you have had a chance to speak with your attorney and your attorney is present.

- **The insurance adjuster is not your friend.**
  It is common practice for insurance adjusters to call injury claimants and attempt to record a statement before the victim has an opportunity to talk to an attorney. The adjuster might seem friendly and sympathetic. But remember, the adjuster is not your friend and is not there to help you. The adjuster actually wants you to make damaging statements so the insurance company can deny your claim and pay you nothing or pay you as little money as possible. Often, the injury victim is still in shock, or even under the influence of medication, and may not be thinking clearly at that time. After an accident, the full extent of your injuries is unknown. It may take days, weeks, months, or longer for all of your injuries to become apparent. The adjuster wants a statement to limit your injury claims. He or she knows full well that taking your statement immediately

Questions? Visit www.fightingforyou.com or call 800-966-4999.

after the accident is premature. So, if you want to fully protect all of your legal rights, under **no** circumstances should you talk to any insurance company, adjuster, representative, investigator, or agent without having an attorney with you.

- **Do not give recorded or written statements to your own insurance company until you speak with a lawyer.** If you are making an uninsured or supplemental underinsured motorist claim (UM/SUM), your own insurance company may use your statement to deny your claim or minimize the amount of money they will pay you. Remember, you are not required to allow the insurance company to record your conversation. In fact, once you tell the insurance company adjuster that you have retained counsel, they are supposed to immediately stop questioning you. In the event they persist, ask the adjuster for their name, phone number, and the claim numbers; tell them your lawyer will call them. If you have any doubts, please consult an attorney immediately.

- **Do not automatically accept the property damage estimate or appraisal of your losses given to you by the insurer.** Insurance companies will often try to get you to accept their own estimator's or contractor's repair or replacement estimates, which could be quite low. **Do not** sign any releases or waivers of any kind until you obtain legal advice. Often the insurance company will base their estimate on cheap replacement parts, and not upon using original equipment manufacturer (OEM) parts. Worse yet, you may think you are signing a release only for property damage;

Questions? Visit www.fightingforyou.com or call 800-966-4999.

however, the release could contain language that includes a release of your bodily injury claim for physical injuries. For these reasons, it is advisable to consult an attorney before signing a release or waiver. Be sure to read the fine print on any payment or release from the insurance company.

- **Do not accept any check from any insurance company that says, "final payment" unless you are ready to settle your entire claim.**
  Be careful not to accept an insurance check for property damage if there is anything on the front or back of the check that indicates it is a final payment or release of all claims. Be aware that this may be a deliberate attempt by the insurance company to trick you into waiving and releasing all your rights.

- **You have thirty (30) days to file for no-fault benefits.**
  Do not ignore time limits set by your own insurance policy. Most policies require a signed application for no-fault personal injury protection benefits (PIP) within thirty (30) days from the date of the accident, or the insurance company may not have to pay you one cent for medical expenses or lost wages. Similarly, if you are injured while at work or actively engaged in a work-related activity, you must give notice to your employer within thirty (30) days or the insurance company may not have to pay your medical bills or lost wages.

- **Most insurance policies require you file a claim for uninsured/supplemental underinsured motorist (UM/SUM) benefits within a certain time limit.**
  In New York State, you have ninety (90) days from the date of the accident to make an UM/SUM claim. The failure to do so could result in the complete loss of your rights.

- **If you are making a claim against any government entity, the deadlines can be as short as thirty (30) days from the date of the injury.**
  If you have any reason to believe your claim may involve a government agency, it is important to contact a lawyer as soon as possible after your accident or you may lose all rights to recover money for the physical injuries you suffered.

- **Do not forget that you have a contract with your insurer.**
  Your insurer has a legal obligation to provide the coverage it promised to you. Be insistent about enforcing that obligation.

- **Do not rely on anything the other driver's insurance company tells you.**
  You **do not** have a contract with the other driver's insurance company, and, in New York, there is no requirement that they treat you fairly. Although the law prohibits insurance companies from acting in bad faith, no insurance company will ever admit to acting in bad faith. The adjuster may or may not be telling you the truth. Understand that the insurance adjuster's job is to protect the insurance company and its own insured driver or property owner. The adjuster has **no** duty to protect you.

The adjuster's job is to pay you nothing or as little as possible in order to get your signature on a release that forever prohibits and bars you from making any additional claims.

- **Do not accept a check or sign a release from the at-fault driver or his or her insurance company until after you have conferred with an attorney.**
  Typically, an attorney will encourage you to wait to accept a check until you have completed your medical treatment, undergone any tests, procedures or surgeries recommended, and your doctor has released you, so you will know that you have received an amount that adequately covers your past and future medical bills and many other damages. An insurance adjuster may push you to settle the claim for the lowest possible amount and may discourage you from contacting an attorney. If so, you should ignore the adjuster's advice and consult an attorney immediately before accepting any payment, signing any release, or otherwise settling your claim. You have to make sure you are receiving fair compensation and not jeopardizing your right to a full and fair recovery.

- **Some injuries take time to develop.**
  Many accident victims accept a fast settlement only to find out later their injuries are far worse than they initially thought. Then later, when they try to get more money, they can't because they already agreed to a settlement. **Do not** make the mistake of settling your claim before knowing the full nature and extent of your injuries. As discussed (and

medical literature supports this), certain injuries take months or years to fully develop and manifest themselves.

- **Do not take advice from anyone other than your experienced personal injury attorney.**
  Don't listen to your friends or neighbors about what you should or shouldn't do. No one has a case exactly like yours, so don't try to compare. It is important that you have an attorney you can trust, have confidence in, and whose advice you can rely on.

- **Once you have retained an experienced personal injury attorney, discuss with your attorney any and all concerns you have** regarding your claim, the litigation process, what you should and shouldn't do, and the value of your case. In the event you don't understand your attorney or the advice is not clear to you, let the attorney know. That is the attorney's fault, not yours.

Fatal Mistake 5: Not Hiring a Lawyer or Hiring the Wrong Lawyer

I mentioned this in passing in previous sections. While it seems that most people should know it is important to seek advice when they are injured, statistics show that many people don't do so. Why? They may not be certain they need a lawyer or are hesitant to speak with one; they may not know how to choose the best lawyer; they may not think they can trust lawyers, or they may mistakenly believe it when the insurance company adjuster tells them that they will end up with less money if they hire an attorney.

In spite of all the lawyer jokes you may have heard, there are many honest, hard-working, and ethical lawyers who can help you deal with an insurance company claim. While it is true that a lawyer will usually get a portion of the money you collect from the insurance company, it is also true that a person represented by a lawyer, on average, receives three and a half times more than a person without a lawyer.

Why is it important to have an attorney in a serious injury claim?

Immediately after sustaining injuries in an accident, you become embroiled in an adversarial legal system. In other words, the insurance company representing the party at fault for the accident has in place a team of adjusters, investigators, and attorneys who are working against you, seeking to pay nothing or as little as possible to settle your claim.

- Many accident victims, already in distressed physical, mental, and financial circumstances, understandably choose to delay what they consider the hassles involved in retaining a personal injury attorney. Some may have had a bad experience with an attorney (in a divorce, for example) or they simply do not like or trust attorneys. Before you make a costly mistake that may ruin your financial future, speak with an experienced, highly credentialed attorney. Their consultation should be free.

- Some accident victims, in an attempt to avoid paying legal fees, try to represent themselves and call an attorney only after the damage has been done. Typically, it is after they have provided recorded statements, filled out forms, and been offered only a nominal sum or had their claim denied altogether. Unfortunately, there are many mistakes (such as providing damaging statements to adjusters) that even the most experienced personal injury attorney cannot "undo." Plus, if you wait too long to get legal help, crucial evidence often disappears, witnesses' memories fade, and you risk losing your claim because the deadlines for filing for benefits or for filing a lawsuit have expired.

- The bottom line is, considering the legalities and complexities of prosecuting a claim for serious personal injury, it is important that you hire an attorney to "level the playing field" and ensure that you receive all the money and benefits you are entitled to.

- As a general rule, you should always hire an attorney in any accident that involves serious injuries. But, if you have been

Questions? Visit www.fightingforyou.com or call 800-966-4999.

In an automobile collision involving property damage only, with no injuries, you probably don't need a lawyer.

- If you didn't contact a lawyer and time has passed, we recommend you contact an attorney immediately to best protect your legal rights.

To summarize, don't wait to hire an attorney. Don't risk losing everything – all the money and benefits you are entitled to – because the time limit to file a claim or bring a lawsuit has expired. Don't lose your right to reimbursement of lost wages, medical expenses, or even your right to file a lawsuit for all the harms and losses you suffered because you didn't contact an attorney in a timely manner.

Choosing the Right Lawyer

Hiring a lawyer is easy. Hiring the right lawyer takes a little extra work. You see, there is as much difference between individual lawyers as there is between doctors, accountants, or other professionals. Choose carefully! It may be the most important decision you make for you and your family's financial future.

Some law firms are personal injury "factories." They simply settle all their cases for much less than the case is worth in order to do as little work as possible or because of their own financial troubles or pressures. They may want to settle quickly simply because they don't know or are not up to date on the law. Others may lack the skill, experience, and financial resources necessary to take on the big insurance companies and win.

Let me suggest that you should stay clear of a situation like that. It's important you retain a law firm that will handle your case from start to finish, will pay personal attention to you, will be available when you need them, and will return your phone calls promptly. Most importantly, you deserve a lawyer that you are comfortable with and have confidence in. You deserve a lawyer that isn't putting on an act but genuinely cares about you and wants to do everything within his or her power to help you as if you were a family member. You are entitled to a lawyer who doesn't talk down to you but listens to you and talks with you, not at you. The right lawyer should provide you with a sense of relief that removes the burden, uncertainty, frustration, and anxiety of not knowing what to do or expect. Hiring the right lawyer will allow you to focus on healing and not dealing with the insurance companies and all their paperwork.

One way to learn about a specific law firm is to ask your friends and neighbors for a recommendation. If someone you know has used that firm in the past and has been satisfied with them, consider it a good recommendation.

At a minimum, go online and look at their Google reviews. Look for quotes that include phrases like these: "made a most difficult situation easier," "provided for the financial security for my family and me for life," "no longer have to worry about anything," "my family's future is secure," "they treated me like family," "I would highly recommend them to family and friends," "an amazing team that helped me at a difficult time," or, "Getting Schwartzapfel Lawyers on my team was the best move I've ever made."

45

Then meet with the lawyers. Not all lawyers are alike. Ask any questions you may have. I want clients to ask questions of me and of the lawyers and employees who work at my firm because I want clients to be confident that they have chosen the best firm for them.

Here are some questions you might consider asking a law firm before hiring them:

1. How much experience does your firm have in representing personal injury clients?
2. Does the firm have a proven track record of success?
3. Can the firm provide testimonials from highly satisfied clients attesting to how they would recommend the law firm to their friends, family, and others they love and care about?
4. How many positive 5-star Google (online) reviews does the firm have?
5. Have you or any of your lawyers been recognized as a Super Lawyer or named on the list of Top 100 Trial Lawyers by the American Trial Lawyers Association, or Top 100 Trial Lawyers by the National Trial Lawyers Association?
6. Have you been recognized in Legal Leaders as a Top-Rated Lawyer by The Wall Street Journal, New York Law Journal, Newsday, American Lawyer, or National Law Journal?
7. Have you ever been recognized as a Top-Rated Lawyer by *New York Magazine* or *Forbes*, or as a Leader in Law by *Newsweek*?

8. Have you and your firm received an AV Peer Review rating from Martindale-Hubbell®, the highest possible rating for both legal ability and ethical standards?

9. Have you and your firm received an A+ rating from the Better Business Bureau?

10. Are you and your lawyers members of the elite Multi-Million Dollar Advocates Forum, a prestigious group of trial lawyers in the United States limited to attorneys who have won multi-million-dollar verdicts and/or settlements?

11. Have you and your firm been featured in the New York Law Journal as having some of the highest verdicts and settlements in the county or state?

12. Have you or any of your lawyers ever served as president, officer, board member, or Dean of any bar association, or lectured to attorneys or judges on the law?

13. Have you ever served on a judicial screening committee?

14. Do you promise to return all calls the same day but in no event later than twenty-four hours?

15. Will you copy me with everything you do on my case?

16. Have you ever been disciplined by the State Bar Association?

17. Has anyone ever sued you for legal malpractice?

18. Do you carry a legal malpractice insurance policy?

19. Will you guarantee your legal fee will not be more than the amount of money I receive?

20. Why should I hire you to represent me?

Important Note:

I have heard many stories of lawyers who will settle a client's personal injury claim and then at the end of all the bookkeeping, the lawyer ends up with more money than the client! This is not how we treat our clients. My law firm never takes a fee that is more than our clients' share of the recovery.

Do not hire a lawyer unless he or she is willing to reduce their attorney fee and expenses so it will **not** be more than your share of the recovery. Otherwise, the lawyer may be tempted to settle a claim just so the lawyer can get paid back his or her expenses and take a full fee, regardless of how much the client receives.

Fatal Mistake 6: Not Being Honest With Your Lawyer

- **Don't try to hide past accidents from your lawyer.**
  Once you begin a case, the other side will be interested in knowing how many past accidents you have had. The reality is that they probably already know the answer or at least have easy access to that information. All insurance companies subscribe to insurance databases that contain records of millions of accident claims, and often the only reason they ask you this question is to test your credibility. If you have been in other accidents, an experienced personal injury attorney knows how to effectively handle this issue. Not telling your lawyer and misrepresenting your accident history to anyone can be fatal to your case.

- **Don't try to hide past injuries from your lawyer.**
  It should go without saying that you need to be up-front and honest with your attorney about any injuries that occurred before or after this particular accident. Again, if you saw a doctor or other healthcare provider, then there is a record in existence that your insurance company will probably find. Your lawyer can deal with this if he or she knows about it. If you lie and the insurance company finds out, then you may receive a much lesser settlement or worse.

- **Don't try to hide any past lawsuits you've had, claims you have made, or moneys received from past settlements.**
  A good lawyer can effectively deal with these issues if he or she knows about them. If you withhold issues such as these from your lawyer, the other side may bring them to your

lawyer's attention at trial. This is not a good thing. A jury will not take kindly to someone not being truthful.

- **Don't misrepresent your income.**
  In many cases, a claimant will have lost income because of the accident. You may only be able to claim that lost income if your past tax returns are correct. You don't want to risk claiming a loss of income, only to have your past tax returns not back you up on your claim. Again, being honest with your attorney is essential, because he or she can deal with the problem if informed about it in advance.

- **Don't misrepresent your activity level.**
  Insurance companies routinely hire private investigators to conduct video surveillance. If you claim that you cannot run, climb, lift or bend, and you get caught on video, you're going to have serious problems. Your testimony must be truthful and your conduct consistent with your testimony. **Always tell the truth.** There is no good explanation that can overcome the eye of the camera. If you have to come up with an excuse or explain a video, you are in trouble. It can destroy your case. You will end up with a much lesser amount or a defense verdict.

- **Don't change your address, telephone, or employment without notifying your attorney.**
  Your lawyer must be able to locate you immediately if an important question or problem arises.

- **Don't try to hide the truth from your lawyer about a past criminal history, or about drug or alcohol abuse.**
  Once again, your lawyer can handle almost any problem if you tell him or her about it. If your lawyer is "ambushed" by the insurance company or defense counsel with such damaging information, your lawyer has no time to prepare a defense. If you had a prior criminal history or drug or alcohol problem, bring it to your lawyer's attention. Remember, a good lawyer is your advocate, not a judge. An experienced attorney knows how best to handle these issues and present them to an adjuster, judge, and jury.

- **Tell your lawyer about every doctor you see.**
  This important information ensures that the nature and extent of your injuries and resultant disabilities are properly known and pled by your lawyer.

- **Don't miss any meeting scheduled with your lawyer.**
  Your time with your lawyer is valuable. There is a purpose for scheduled meetings. Sometimes a meeting can be rescheduled, but other times a meeting is time sensitive and critical.

- **Don't skip over any letter from your lawyer and do call if there is something in it you don't understand.**
  Sometimes a letter is just to tell you that your case is progressing normally and the letter is, frankly, not too important. But other times, a letter gives you essential information or informs you about an important deadline in your case.

Questions? Visit www.fightingforyou.com or call 800-966-4999.

Fatal Mistake 7: Exaggerating Your Injuries or Not Being Completely Honest In Other Ways

- **You have no idea how much information the insurance company has about you.**
  The best way to ruin your claim is to lie or try to hide something such as how badly you're hurt, what you can no longer do as a result of your injuries, or to deny you were previously injured or treated for the same or similar injuries. They will find out if you lie about one little thing, and then they won't believe anything else you say. This is especially true of injuries. One lie, even about a small matter, can kill your case.

- **Insurance companies have access to any past injury claims you have made—auto, job, and other; criminal records; marriages, divorces, and past addresses, etc.**
  They may park outside your house to video your comings and goings. I have seen insurance company surveillance tapes of my clients taking out the trash, gardening, washing the car, going to the beach, walking, trying to work out, etc. The insurance companies always try to say my clients aren't really hurt because they can perform these simple activities. There's a big difference between doing a task once and having to do it repetitively all day long. Tell us the truth and we will handle it, whatever it is.

- **Insurance companies have access to your social media posts.**
  Always tell the truth. There is no better way to destroy your case than to lie and deny something you did and then have

a jury watch a video of you doing what you testified you cannot do. Everyone can understand a person trying to do something he or she once loved doing or a person having to do something because no one else was available to do it, despite the medication or pain suffered later. No one will tolerate or accept a bold-faced liar. Have I made this simple point clear? **Always tell the truth**.

- **Do be honest and forthcoming with your lawyer.**
  Even if it may seem embarrassing, it is better if your lawyer knows all the facts. Failing to be candid with your lawyer can ruin any potential claim you may have and give the defendant a defense that they may not have otherwise had.

Questions? Visit www.fightingforyou.com or call 800-966-4999.

Fatal Mistake 8: Oversharing on Social Media

When you are involved in an accident and are pursuing an injury claim, it is strongly suggested that you not be active on social media. Anything that you post can be found by the insurance company and be used against you. Posting anything on social media after an accident can be very detrimental to your claim and recovery for damages. What you post can be taken out of context, misconstrued, and used against you. I have included on the next page a copy of a letter we send out routinely to our new clients. It has some good advice on this topic.

Dear Client: Be Silent on Social Media

If you belong to a public social networking account such as Facebook, Twitter, YouTube, etc., we STRONGLY recommend that you close it until your case is complete.

If you choose not to close your accounts, we warn you to use great caution. Whatever you write or post, or have written or posted, will probably fall into the hands of the defense attorney or insurance company. It is now standard practice for these agencies to run computer searches and investigations to obtain information about your personal life. They will try to obtain it without your knowledge or permission. Increasingly, they will demand that you provide them with your account passwords. They will also ask the court to order release of your password information.

If you have such a site, you should immediately verify all your settings are on PRIVATE (the highest setting possible) and nothing is public. Even with the highest privacy settings, you should only write or post items that cannot be used to hurt you. These sites are open to the public. The law is unclear if or to what extent privacy laws apply.

Our best advice to you is that you take down your sites until your case is over. We understand you may decide to keep your site(s). If so, we make the following recommendations. DO NOT:

- Allow anyone to become a "friend" unless you are absolutely certain you know the person
- Post any photographs or video of yourself (or enable others to "tag" you)
- Write or disclose anything about your personal life that you would be embarrassed to have a defense attorney use against you in front of a judge or jury
- Send emails regarding your case to anyone except your attorneys
- Send texts regarding your case to anyone except your attorneys
- Participate in blogs, chat rooms, or message boards

We understand limiting your social networking is a great inconvenience; however, we have found that almost anything you do or say can be misconstrued and used against you.

Respectfully,

Schwartzapfel Lawyers P.C.

55

Questions? Visit www.fightingforyou.com or call 800-966-4999.

The Claims and Litigation Process

A lawsuit begins by filing a summons and complaint with the court and serving the defendant with a copy of the same. The defendant then has a limited time to serve an answer. In the event the defense attorney fails to serve an answer, we then have to apply to the court for a default judgment. Typically, the defendant will then serve his or her answer, which always denies all allegations of wrongdoing.

Thereafter, the plaintiff (the person suing) and the defendant (the person, party, or entity being sued) engage in discovery. This is the phase of the litigation where the defendant demands copies of every record or document related to your claim including police reports, witness statements, accident reports, photos, and hospital, medical, health provider, school, employment, and income tax records.

During the discovery phase, the plaintiff will demand information the defendant or its insurance company may have that would help maximize our client's financial recovery. This includes information related to the defendant's investigation of the case. For example, the plaintiff will demand copies of any photographs or surveillance taken of the plaintiff. The plaintiff may also demand witness statements, incident reports, and insurance coverage information. Depending on who the defendants are, we may make specialized demands. In a trucking accident case, for example, the plaintiff may demand records related to the employment driving history of the truck driver, safety inspections and violations of the truck, time logs, and other information relevant to the case.

Questions? Visit www.fightingforyou.com or call 800-966-4999.

Next, the defendant will typically demand and conduct an examination of you under oath. This is called a deposition, and you will be asked questions related to the accident and your injuries. Although it's natural to be anxious, remember you were not at fault, you were not the wrongdoer. All that you will do is tell the truth. It is your lawyer's job to spend the time and prepare you for the deposition, so you have a certain comfort level.

The questions will primarily be about the incident, your injuries, and the losses you sustained. We will also conduct discovery of the defendant, which includes obtaining records and taking the defendant's deposition.

The defendant may also demand that you undergo medical examination(s) by doctors the defendant's insurance company chooses. These doctors are not there to help you; their sole purpose is to minimize or deny your injuries are serious or related to this accident. Please don't be surprised by this, it is to be expected and an experienced attorney is familiar with these tactics and knows how to effectively deal with them.

After all discovery is completed, we file the appropriate papers and place the case on the trial calendar. We have to wait our turn for trial. The waiting time for trial varies from county to county. While waiting for trial, the judge will conduct one or more pre-trial conferences to try to settle the case. If the case does not settle at this point, we proceed to trial where a jury will determine fault and money damages.

Questions? Visit www.fightingforyou.com or call 800-966-4999.

The vast majority of all cases settle before going to trial, but it is important to have a law firm with the skill, experience, and financial resources to go to verdict in the event the insurance company is unreasonable. The insurance companies and defense lawyers know which law firms have a proven track record of success. They know which law firms have the skills, experience, expertise, and financial resources to take verdicts and win. Remember, the reputation of your attorney makes a huge difference in the amount of money you may ultimately receive.

Frequently Asked Questions

What is my case worth?

Any lawyer who gives an opinion as to the specific value of the case without the benefits of fully and completely investigating and reviewing every item of liability as well as damages is either inexperienced, incompetent, inept, or desperate.

Each and every case is different and a competent, experienced lawyer will spend the time, money, and resources to conduct a thorough investigation. The lawyer will obtain and review every single document, record, and report; they will retain appropriate experts and review the applicable law prior to rendering an opinion as to the value of the case. To do otherwise is a disservice to the client.

After careful consideration and evaluation of your case, an experienced lawyer should be able to give you a range of what your case is worth based upon the specific facts of your case, the applicable law, and previous cases he or she has handled with similar liability as well as damages.

How much money will I receive?

The amount of money you may ultimately collect, whether by settlement or verdict, will vary depending upon many factors. These factors include, but are not limited to:

- Liability and Damages—how the accident occurred, your available proof, photographs, video, witness statements, experts' opinions on liability, and experts' opinions on damages. Some examples of experts may include, but not be limited to: accident reconstruction, biomechanics, doctors, economists, life care planners, and/or vocational rehabilitation experts.

- The nature and extent of your injuries, resultant disability, and other damages sustained, such as past and future medical expenses, may include hospital, rehab, physical therapy, medical devices, household services, lost wages, loss of pension, loss of annuity, and loss of Social Security benefits.
- The state and county where the action is pending, as well as the judge assigned, are significant factors regarding the value of your claim.
- Lastly, regardless of how seriously injured you are and how substantial the damages suffered, the ultimate amount of money you may receive will be limited to the amount of available insurance coverage and/or by the amount of money the Appellate Court has previously upheld or sustained for similar injuries and losses suffered.

The reputation your attorney has with the defense lawyers and insurance companies makes a huge difference in the amount of money you may ultimately receive whether by settlement or verdict.

What happens if the insurance company says my car is totaled?

If the cost to repair the vehicle is 75% or more than the value of the car, most insurance companies may "total" the vehicle and give you a check for what they believe the car is worth. In the event you financed the car and the amount of money the insurance company pays you is less than the amount owed the bank, you may end up with no car but with an obligation to continue paying for it anyway (you didn't borrow the car from the bank; you borrowed the money). For situations like this, there is a type of insurance coverage called guaranteed auto protection (GAP) insurance. You can often purchase this type of protection when you buy or lease a new car.

What if the person who caused the accident doesn't have insurance?

If the person at fault does not have coverage for the damage he or she has caused to you, you may have to file an injury claim under your own insurance policy. This coverage is referred to as uninsured motorist (UM) insurance and is included in every policy in New York. The minimum policy limits are $25,000, however, it can be much higher depending on the premium paid. We cannot emphasize enough how very important it is that you make certain you have the highest uninsured motorist coverage available. It is one of the least expensive insurances offered in New York. We strongly recommend that you have minimum UM limits of $500,000. As previously mentioned, the average person will be in auto three accidents in their lifetime. Make certain you and your family are protected. Saving a couple hundred dollars but losing $500,000 in coverage is a horrible thing to allow to happen. Usually, one dollar per week buys $100,000 of UM coverage. Please see the insurance definitions section of the book for more detail.

What is No-Fault insurance?

No-Fault coverage pays for reasonable and necessary medical expenses and lost wages for covered parties for treatment due

61

to injuries sustained in an automobile accident. This coverage applies regardless of whether or not you are responsible for the accident and includes passengers in your vehicle or even pedestrians injured by your vehicle during an automobile accident.

New York State's No-Fault Law was passed in 1973 and amended in 1977. Its purpose was to rid the court system of minor neck/back sprain/strain-type injuries that were clogging the courts.

Before No-Fault, if you were stopped at a light and hit on the rear bumper, you would have to sue the driver and owner of the other car to collect your lost wages and medical expenses.

Under No-Fault, you no longer have to sue the other driver to recover your losses. Even though the accident was no fault of yours, your insurance company will pay your medical expenses, lost wages, and other reasonable and necessary expenses related to the accident and pursuant to the applicable policy.

What is PIP insurance?
PIP (personal injury protection) coverage provides up to $50,000 for medical bills, increased household expenses such as housekeeping or transportation ($25/day for up to one year), 80% of lost earnings up to $2,000 a month for 3 years, and a $2,000 death benefit. You may have more coverage called Supplemental PIP benefits. Ask your lawyer about this.

How are my medical bills paid and what is my obligation?
In New York, No-Fault insurance covers medical bills related to an accident. You are required to file the claim within thirty (30)

Questions? Visit www.fightingforyou.com or call 800-966-4999.

days. Failure to do so may result in the insurance company not having to pay one cent.

Simply stated, you MUST file a completed No-Fault application within the prescribed thirty (30)-day period. Failure to do so may result in a denial from the insurance company for any and all medical expenses and lost wages.

What is an Independent Medical Exam (IME)?

It is an examination by a doctor chosen and hired by the insurance company. It is not truly an independent examination. It is paid for by the insurance company. As such, most IME exams result in a denial of continued treatment. Upon denial, the insurance company will no longer pay for any medical expenses or loss of wages.

If you receive a notice scheduling a date for your IME, you may reschedule one time. If you fail to appear for the rescheduled IME, the insurance company will stop paying No-Fault benefits automatically. You are not allowed to reschedule an IME more than once.

What if I have already hired another attorney to handle my case? Can I change lawyers?

Our firm normally does not accept a case in which another attorney has been involved, and we do not want to interfere with any legal relationship you may presently have. In the event you already have a lawyer and this book has raised certain questions or concerns, we suggest you speak to your current lawyer and discuss your questions and concerns with him or her. Law often involves judgment calls. Each lawyer does things a little differently, and those differences do not mean that we are right and your lawyer is wrong.

When your lawyer returns your call and answers your questions, make certain you understand the answers. Ask yourself if the answer the lawyer gave you makes sense. We advise our clients to ask questions, and if they do not understand the answers, it is the fault of the lawyers, not the clients'. We encourage lawyers to talk to their clients in plain English. Hopefully after sitting down with your lawyer and discussing your concerns, you have a better sense of confidence in him or her.

Statement of Client's Rights

At Schwartzapfel Lawyers, you have the following rights:

1. To be treated with courtesy, consideration, dignity and respect by every Schwartzapfel Lawyer and our personnel.
2. To have your questions and concerns addressed promptly and to talk to your lawyer the same day you call.
3. To be updated regularly and kept informed as to the progress and status of your matter.
4. To have a highly qualified and well-credentialed lawyer capable of handling your matter competently and diligently in accordance with the highest legal and ethical standards of the profession.
5. To have your lawyer's independent judgment and individual loyalty uncompromised by conflicts of interest.
6. To maintain privacy in your dealings with your lawyer and have your secrets and confidences preserved and protected to the fullest extent of the law.
7. To only pay a fee if we win money for you, as set forth in a written fee agreement.
8. To have your legitimate objectives respected by your lawyer, including whether or not to settle your case.
9. To have your client-share of the recovery be more than your lawyer's fee and disbursements.
10. We are here to help you. We are so convinced of our ability to provide you the highest quality client service in a timely manner that we guarantee it. If during the first thirty (30) days you are not completely satisfied with our services, you may discharge us, ask us for your file back, and owe us no attorney fees.

Questions? Visit www.fightingforyou.com or call 800-966-4999.

Automobile Insurance Definitions

It is important that you have a basic understanding of the various types of insurance coverage available to you so that you can better protect yourself and your family. It will also provide you with a better understanding of the fatal mistakes that can destroy your accident claim.

These are simplified, plain-language descriptions of the most common types of auto insurance, terms and how they may benefit you. Although at first glance they may seem boring, when you realize that the terms and types of coverage will determine the amount of money and benefits you can recover, they aren't so boring!

Bodily Injury Limits

If you are driving your car and you hit and cause bodily injury to another person due to your carelessness, negligence, and/or fault, this coverage protects you when the injured person makes a claim or files a lawsuit against you. This coverage requires your insurance company to defend the claim and indemnify, which means to pay the injured person such sum as negotiated or awarded by a judge or jury up to the policy limits. The amount of coverage you choose and the premium you pay caps the amount the insurance company is obligated to pay.

For example, if your bodily injury limits are the New York minimum of 25/50, your insurance company will pay no more than $25,000 to one person, no matter how badly injured that person may be. The total amount the insurance company will pay is $50,000 dollars regardless of how many people are injured. If you hit and injured three people and your insurance company paid one person $25,000 dollars, the remaining two injured people would have to split the remaining $25,000.

You will be personally liable for any money damages awarded above the amount of your bodily injury limits. Other bodily injury liability insurance limits may be 100/300, 250/500, and $500,000 and higher.

Property Damage Liability

This is similar to bodily injury liability except that it covers damage to another person's vehicle and property rather than physical injuries. The company's obligation to pay is also limited to the amount of coverage you buy. The minimum limit for property damage coverage in New York is $10,000. Of course, $10,000 doesn't come close to repairing a badly damaged new vehicle these days, so we always recommend that our clients purchase additional coverage. It's surprisingly inexpensive to increase your liability coverage above the minimum required by law.

Comprehensive

This category of protection generally requires your insurance company to pay for damage to your car caused by something other than an auto accident, for example: fire, theft, or vandalism.

The amount of any "deductible" you have also limits the company's obligation to you. A $500 deductible means that you pay the first $500; the company pays the rest up to the policy limits you bought.

Collision Coverage

This coverage requires your insurance company to pay for damage to your car, regardless of whose fault it was. If you have collision coverage and you were not at fault—for instance, while stopped, another car hit your car from behind—the other car's insurance company (if the owner has any insurance) is not legally required to automatically pay for the damage to your car. With collision coverage, your insurance company pays for your damage, even if the accident wasn't your fault. Your insurance company then pursues your claim against the other driver and his or her insurance company. This way you don't have to spend the time or hire a lawyer to collect from the other driver. Your insurance company's obligation is to pay for your property damage less the amount of any deductible you may have. For instance, a $500 deductible means that you pay the first $500, the insurance company pays the rest up to the amount of coverage you bought.

Personal Injury Protection Coverage

Personal injury protection, or "PIP" for short, means your insurance company will pay the medical expenses for anyone in your car who sustained injuries in an accident. Even though the accident may have been no fault of yours, New York law requires that your insurance company pay for the medical expense of anyone in your car up to the NYS "PIP" minimum limits of $50,000 per person, regardless of how many occupants were injured.

This coverage also protects you and most family members of your household for medical expenses if you were a pedestrian struck by an unknown or uninsured car. We always recommend that our clients increase their PIP limits above the minimum required by the law, as it is relatively inexpensive.

The Most Critical Coverages to Have

1. Uninsured Motorist Coverage

This is one of the most important insurance coverages that you can purchase to protect you and your family. "UM" coverage protects you and most family members in the event a driver causes injuries to you or your car's occupants and has no car insurance.

This coverage in effect wraps around and provides liability coverage to the uninsured car so that you may file a personal injury claim, even though the car was uninsured. This coverage serves as a substitute for the bodily injury liability insurance that the other driver did not have.

In today's economic environment it is reported that as many as 20 percent of the vehicles on the road are uninsured. In New York State, the statutory minimum is $25,000. It is not uncommon for us to see clients with 100/300 bodily injury limits and only $25,000 of uninsured motorist "UM" coverage.

In this example you are providing $100,000 coverage per person and $300,000 total to strangers that you may have accidentally injured, but you and your own family have only $25,000 available to cover your injuries if hit by an uninsured or hit-and-run driver. The insurance company would rather you not know about uninsured motorist coverage, as it is the least expensive insurance in New York State.

We strongly recommend and urge you to immediately call your insurance company or insurance broker and increase your uninsured motorist coverage to $500,000 or at least equal to your bodily injury limits. Call us if any of this is unclear.

In the event you have any questions or concerns regarding your insurance policy and the appropriate coverages to best protect you and your family, call and speak to me or one of the other attorneys in my office, completely free of charge and without obligation. The number is 800-966-4999.

2. Underinsured Motorist Coverage

If a driver injures you, your family members, or your car's occupants, and the at-fault driver's liability insurance is insufficient to cover the full value of your claims for physical injuries, this coverage will make up the difference up to the policy limits. Supplementary underinsured motorist coverage, "SUM" for short, is the name of this insurance.

For example, if the driver seriously injures you but only has the NYS minimum bodily injury limits of 25/50, the most you or any one person in your car can recover from the driver's insurance company is $25,000 dollars. If you had supplementary underinsured motorist coverage of $250,000 dollars, your insurance company would provide an additional $225,000 to cover your claims for physical injuries.

We recommend you immediately purchase the maximum amount of UM/SUM coverage you can afford. Certain insurance carriers offer UM/SUM with limits exceeding one million dollars. Remember, it is the least expensive insurance coverage you can purchase to protect you and your family. No one ever thinks they will be seriously injured; however, according to the National Highway Transportation Safety Administration's latest data, more than 100 people die and over 7,500 people are injured in auto accidents every day.[2] Don't delay, purchase this additional UM/SUM coverage today. It is surprisingly inexpensive.

3. Spousal Coverage

Let's face it, we don't typically drive with strangers in our cars; more often we drive with our spouses (meaning your husband or wife). Up until recently you could not buy spousal coverage in New York State. Before the law changed, if you sustained serious injuries in an accident as a result of your spouse's careless driving, there was no insurance coverage to cover your claims for physical injuries.

Today we urge you to check your policy to make certain you have spousal coverage. Your failure to do so can have horrible consequences for you and your family. Don't wait. Call your insurance company or insurance broker to purchase spousal coverage.

Hopefully this information has taken some of the mystery out of the different types of insurance coverage available to protect you, your family and loved ones.

In the event you have any questions or concerns regarding your insurance policy and the appropriate coverages to best protect you and your family, please call us at 800-966-4999.

---

[2] https://crashstats.nhtsa.dot.gov

Summary

I hope this book has provided some truly valuable information. You now know how insurance companies operate and what you can do from the beginning to best protect yourself, your family, and how to maximize the money and benefits you are entitled to.

Insurance companies exist to make profits for their shareholders. The insurance company's business is to take in premiums and pay out as little money in claims as possible. Despite all of the many tips and suggestions provided to you in this book, you may still feel overwhelmed, anxious, scared, or simply uncertain as to what to do next. We find that our clients feel substantially better after speaking with us.

Don't allow the insurance company to intimidate or bully you into giving statements, signing documents, or settling your case without first seeing a lawyer. To do so could be the worst decision of your life.

Do not allow the insurance company to pressure or threaten you. The insurance companies know that a person represented by a lawyer receives, on average, three and a half times more money than a person without legal representation. You can't make the best decision if you are being pressured and have not spoken to a lawyer.

After having represented thousands of clients, I can assure you they feel substantially better after speaking to us regarding their accident, injuries, and how we can best protect their legal rights. We get our clients the money and benefits they are entitled to. When you come to our office, ask to meet the team

Questions? Visit www.fightingforyou.com or call 800-966-4999.

of lawyers, paralegals, and support staff to see the resources and technology at our disposal.

Go online and review firsthand the hundreds of 5-star Google reviews attesting to how Schwartzapfel Lawyers changed their lives, provided for their financial security, made a most difficult situation easier, and treated them like family.

In the event you were seriously injured and cannot come to us, we will arrange for transportation to our office or make certain we come to you to discuss your case and talk about your rights. We will make certain you are aware of all the money and benefits you may be entitled to.

Consultations are free of charge. There is absolutely no obligation. We do this because we are genuinely interested in helping people. It is important that you have a lawyer you are comfortable with and have confidence in. We welcome the opportunity to speak with you.

It is important that you act sooner rather than later. **Waiting to speak to a lawyer is good for the insurance company and bad for you.** The insurance company will do whatever they can to convince you not to see a lawyer. Meanwhile, the clock is ticking and the insurance companies have teams of law firms protecting their interests. The longer you wait to speak to a lawyer, the greater the likelihood that you will not receive all the money and benefits you are entitled to. Evidence is lost, witnesses will move, memories fade, and the time to file or make a claim for money and benefits may expire. The longer you wait, the more stress you will be under, the greater the likelihood that you will do or fail to do something that will harm your case. Remember, there are strict time limits to apply for benefits, make claims. and file lawsuits. Don't gamble with your family's future. Allow Schwartzapfel Lawyers the privilege of handling your case so you may focus on your health and recovery. Take action today and call us now at 800-966-4999.

Why Choose Schwartzapfel Lawyers to Represent You?

For more than thirty-five years, Schwartzapfel Lawyers has successfully helped thousands of people get the money and benefits they are entitled to. We are proud of our proven track record of getting our clients the money and benefits they deserve, which has resulted in our 99% client satisfaction rating.

Please take a few moments to review the Statement of Client's Rights on page 65. It sets forth not only our commitment to you, but reiterates our 30-day, no-risk guarantee.

We Work on Contingency

Schwartzapfel Lawyers only gets paid if we get you money. We have every incentive to get you the largest settlement or verdict possible, as quickly as possible. If we don't win your case, you owe us nothing.

Schwartzapfel Lawyers made a decision not to be the biggest law firm or to represent every person injured as a result of someone else's wrongdoing or someone else's failure to follow the rules. Because we only represent a limited number of clients, we are able to provide exceptional service and obtain among the highest verdicts and settlements in New York State year after year, as reported by the *New York Law Journal*. Contact us today to see how we might help you.

Contact Schwartzapfel Lawyers

I want to thank you for taking the time to read this book. I hope you found this information helpful. If you still have any questions or concerns, please feel free to contact my office at the number below or send us an email. Remember, it's free.

If you have a friend or relative you think might enjoy a copy of the book, just provide their name and mailing address and I will make certain they receive their own copy.

Steven J. Schwartzapfel
Schwartzapfel Lawyers P.C.
600 Old Country Road
Suite 450
Garden City, NY 11530
Phone: 800-966-4999
Email: info@fightingforyou.com
www.fightingforyou.com

Notes

Questions? Visit www.fightingforyou.com or call 800-966-4999.

Notes

Questions? Visit www.fightingforyou.com or call 800-966-4999.